Prai

Reading the introduction to this book, it felt as if I was sipping
water at a pristine spring in the most exquisite of deserts. The poems
sustained the spell, singing the simplicity of a soul fully present to
each magic moment in what is without doubt a most sacred place.
—Dolores Brandon, Author and Journalist

Howard Stein is a master of his craft, one of the brightest minds of
our generation; poetry is in his blood and soul. His sensitivity,
thoughtfulness, and images are as breathtaking and inspiring as the
mesa itself.
—Peter W. Petschauer, Author, Poet, Editor, Professor Emeritus

Presence

Presence
Poems from Ghost Ranch
Howard F. Stein

Golden Word Books
Santa Fe, NM

Unpublished Poems
"Beneath Old Cottonwood"
"Desolation"
"Getting My Bearings"
"Gift of Stillness"
"In Preparation"
"Let Go the Day"
"Viewpoint"
"Writing the Same Poem"

Library of Congress Control Number 2020937179

Published by Golden Word Books, Santa Fe, New Mexico.
www.GoldenWordBooks.com

ISBN 978-1-948749-72-5

*For Ed Knop, with
friendship and gratitude*

Contents

Acknowledgments

I wish to thank many people for their encouragement over two and a half decades of my writing poems from Ghost Ranch, New Mexico: Ed Knop, Deward Walker Jr., Richard Stoffle, Lenora Bohren, Arthur Campa, Peter Van Arsdale, Stephen Stewart, Jack Schultz, Shawn Kelley, David Piacenti, Josef Garrett, Seth Allcorn, Peter Petschauer, Madelyn Eastlund, Johanna Shapiro, David Fraser, Julie Damerell, Nathan Gunter, Annmarie Lockhart, Marla Jones, Layne Kalbfleisch, Steven Wittenberg Gordon, M.D., Dolores Brandon, and many other people.

Introduction: Presence, and the Sense of Place

I HAVE BEEN ATTENDING THE ANNUAL FALL RETREAT OF THE HIGH Plains Society for Applied Anthropology at Ghost Ranch, outside Abiquiu in northern New Mexico, for as long as I can remember, perhaps twenty-five or more years. Months before the actual meeting, I rehearse the trip in my mind, remembering with fondness past retreats, and eagerly anticipating the coming one. I search through Google and study dozens of photographs of Ghost Ranch and the surrounding grassy fields, mesas, spires, and mountains—and the immense sky that crowns the sense of place.

I often begin writing poems about Ghost Ranch in the airport as I start the return trip to my home in Oklahoma City. The writing continues for several weeks. In recent years, I have even begun writing poems in the weeks before actually being in the physical Presence of the place. Yet the word *physical* does injustice, even moral violence, to Ghost Ranch. It is not simply a collection of stone *objects* on a monumental scale and the tiniest, most delicate high desert flowers. Physical objects are only points of departure, and do not have the final say. They become hints, metaphors, allegories, gentle pointers. A line from Walt Whitman's poem *Miracles*, in *Leaves of Grass*, comes to mind: "As to me, I know of nothing else but miracles."

Ghost Ranch, as place and people, renews me every year. It is never the same, always refreshing and surprising and astonishing me. Each visit yields discovery and imbues me with wonder. For me, the Sense of Place that Ghost Ranch evokes is *Presence*. And with *Presence*, awe and gratitude.

Owned and run by the Presbyterian Church since 1955, Ghost Ranch is about sixty-five miles northwest of Santa Fe. Situated at the eastern end of the Colorado Plateau, it is part of the Piedra Lumbre basin ("Valley of the Shining Stone," specifically, quartz), once a Spanish land grant. Characterized by numerous largely sandstone mesas with parallel layered and multi-colored strata, the region was spared the violent uplifting and folding of the Rio Grande Rift to the east. Nearby mountains include Cerro Pedernal, a slanted, flat-topped ancient volcano that inspired many famous paintings by long-time Ghost Ranch resident Georgia O'Keeffe.

Ghost Ranch consists of twenty-one thousand acres of mesas, buttes, canyons, gorges, spires, steep cliffs, grasslands, plains, the Arroyo del Meso, the Chama River, and much more. More than 165 million years ago, it was part of a shallow inland sea near the equator, and home to dinosaurs and ferns. Today, it is high desert—it may be arid but it is not devoid of life. It is home to ponderosa pine, piñon pine, juniper, cottonwood, mesquite, Gambel oak/scrub oak, blue gamma grass, chamisa (rubber rabbitbrush), sagebrush, and numerous species of hearty wildflowers. Its history spans more than 200 million years.

Ghost Ranch's lodgings and other buildings are rustic and designed to blend into the vast landscape, not compete with it. The retreat center attracts writers, artists, poets, musicians, spiritual pilgrims, philosophers, hikers, and others who come as individuals, couples, families, and groups, often for year-round workshops, conferences, retreats, and tours ranging from archaeological dinosaur sites to O'Keeffe's home. Except for the incursion of occasional dramatic thunderstorms, Ghost Ranch is a quiet, serene, meditative, and creative space.

Its immensity, its sense of both vastness and enclosure, its grandeur, its sedimentary cliffs' ever-changing color with the angle of the sun, its uninterrupted sky, and its hundreds of millions of years of history, have inspired me and my poetry since my first visit. Ghost Ranch is the most spiritual place I have been. The rocks may be inanimate, but they are not dead. Ghost Ranch is inexhaustible in its gifts. It keeps bringing me back for sustenance and renewal. Over the years, I have written more than a hundred poems in which the setting and mood are those of Ghost Ranch.

More than experiencing Ghost Ranch as an "it"—an object altogether external to me—I find myself in an ongoing intimate *relationship* with Ghost Ranch, as a kind of *Thou* in Martin Buber's theology. For me, Ghost Ranch is both sacred space and sanctuary. My Ghost Ranch trips are pilgrimages, less as escapes from the hectic world of daily commerce and more as reaffirmation of What Is Real in Life—an extraordinary *time* to take back to my ordinary life. Ghost Ranch hints at Supreme Value in life, space and sky and stone as allusion. For me, it is the place where Immanence and Transcendence meet—the Sublime manifest and realized. I think of theologian Dietrich Bonhöffer's phrase, "the Beyond in the midst."

Over many years, my dear friend and colleague, Dr. Ed Knop, an applied anthropologist/sociologist, and member of the High Plains Society, has tutored me in his vast knowledge of New Mexico peoples, history, geography, and geology. I owe to him much of my historical grounding in Ghost Ranch. He has long encouraged me to explore my lived experience of Ghost Ranch through poetry. I dedicate this book to him and to our long friendship.

Several years ago, he highly recommended a book to me which I now re-read before my annual trips to northern New Mexico: *Ghost Ranch* by Lesley Poling-Kempes. It is part of my psychological and spiritual preparation for the retreat. What Poling-Kempes writes about the "theology of place" rings true to what happens to me when I am in the *Presence* of Ghost Ranch. As a poet and grateful sojourner, I hope the poems in this book evoke that Presence for you.

Howard F. Stein
June 2020

High Desert Valley

The long valley is inexhaustible;
no set of eyes can possess it—
tens of thousands of acres
of high desert grass and chamisa
nested between mesas and far mountains.
I stand transfixed
by a place more vast
than my expansive ego.

The land conquers me;
I surrender to the long valley
without resistance.
It stakes its claim
upon my willing soul.
I am gratefully possessed.

Mesas and Mountains

Steep mesas and wide mountains
reckon time in measures
my rushed days cannot parse.
Geologic cliches,
redeemed by awe,
temper claims of
triumph's duration—
all vanity
faces extinction.
In mesas and mountains,
I did not find eternity,
but what I found
was time enough.

Skyward

The Earth
begins as geography
and ends as sky.

Above the Piedra Lumbre basin
and the Chama River Valley,
above the Cliffs of Shining Stone,
above the high desert that spans forever,
dwells a more immense forever
where the Milky Way nearly blinds you by night,
where you can follow the sun's long arc by day,
where you can see sprawling storms in their far approach—

the realm of sky,
more than an eye can hold,
more than arms can wrap around,
more than imagination can grasp—
spawning wave upon wave
of terror and reassurance,
desolation and comfort,
exposure and enclosure;
where we give names to stars
and group them into familiars
so we don't leak out into infinity—
constellations, our celestial mesas and buttes,
to give bounds to the badlands of our minds,
as if the sky could at last have a skin,
and we could fall asleep under the stars
and not be afraid.

Gift of Stillness

If I could give you
stillness,
I would give you
a crisp fall evening,
Cassiopeia rising in the east
above the mesa,
the air an almost
reverent hush,
the last light of dusk
peering through the trees,
and a gentle mist
of cottonwood leaves
drifting downward sleepily,
in no hurry
to reach the ground.

Geology Lesson
for Ed Knop

plateau
mesa
butte
pinnacle
chimney rock
cap rock—
surfaces of the past,

sedimentary layers
iced with hard lava,
eons that give
a new slant to our ambition.
Here time stands still
not even a second.
Water, ice, and wind
have work to do,
proclaiming their sovereignty
over geology's fleeting majesty.

Still, I marvel,
knowing full well
that erosion is just
another word for time.

Measure

Mesas, mountains,
canyons, valleys, sky—
transmute unimaginable
into imaginable
sense of place
but preserve
the scale and miracle
of ineffable space.

Getting My Bearings

I have lost my bearings—
where am I? Where *all* am I
at once?
I stand on the valley floor,
steep mesas to my back and side.
My eyes stretch far ahead,
from grassland to mist
and mountain,
then sky, only sky, not above
and beyond,
but a crown of time upon earthly time.
Mesas are tricksters, remnants
of layer upon layer of sediment
crushed into rock.
I, in the valley, gaze toward the top
of the mesas, once the bottom
of a vast sea. My mind spins;
I am standing on rocks
far beneath an ocean.
Dinosaurs roamed and clashed
far above me in bloody battle.
The sea is long gone except
in a lively imagination that reels
with "Where am I, now and then
and simultaneously?" How beguiling
this landscape where far off time
and far off space merge
in a mind that reaches way around
to grasp it all in a single sweep.
A brisk wind ruffles another sea—
a symphony of yellow

cottonwood leaves,
reminds me of yet another season.
I am in all these places and times;
I have my bearings again.

Inanimate But Not Dead

Inanimate mesas,
buttes, and spires,
stories and storytellers
in stone,
lack lungs, larynx,
vocal cords, tongue, and mouth
but still give voice
to mute rock formations.
This is the epic
Homer would have told if he
had been made of sandstone,
siltstone, mudstone, quartz,
and cooled lava flow.
Sagas of life
sealed in the silent rock
of ruddy escarpments
that glow at sunset.
Inanimate rocks
are not dead;
they never cease
to tell their stories.
Listen now—
they are speaking.

Cottonwood Leaves in Autumn

Across the parched hayfield,
A stand of old cottonwoods
Lines the banks of a mostly
Languid arroyo.
Come late September,
We can hardly wait
For the first cold snap,
When summer's ripe green leaves
Abruptly change to brilliant yellow.

Of the many ways of reckoning time,
We mark ours by fall's alchemy
Of cottonwood's color—
Transmutation of leaves
Through a shift in the direction
Of Earth's tilt
In its journey around the sun.

How odd, that when
Explanation should suffice,
We nonetheless welcome
This transposition in color
As if a loved one
Had just returned home?

Fugitive Hues

On the mesa's steep face,
On the canyon's deep walls,
Each slight change
In the sun's angle
Provokes a new color
For which no name
Can be found.
The tone vanishes before
It can be fixed in sound.

So swiftly do colors
Arrive and depart,
The largest box
Of children's crayons
Could not contain
Sandstone's story
Of daily rhythm
In this high desert sun—

Futile to try to pin down
In words
Fleeting color,
Fleeting time,
Each glance,
Both a perishing
And a renewal.

A Mesa and Its Moon

A gibbous moon ascends
As a faint haze above
The blinding face of the
Sheer sandstone cliff,
Lit by a late afternoon sun.
As the moon rises toward night,
Sky darkens; brilliant colors
Of the mesa fade into shadow
And vanish.
A now-blinding moon
Rules the sky—
Moon and mesa,
Partners in a conversation between
Darkness and light,
Appearing and disappearing
To the strong pulse
Of this exalted place.

Three Layers of Night

for Layne Kalbfleisch

Below—a cold, blustery night
on a high desert that was once a sea.

Above—stars float like fish
in the steady rotation of the sky-bowl.

Beyond—violent interstellar winds
swirl hot gasses in the birthplace of stars,
and old white dwarfs explode into oblivion.

Three layers,
a single mind.

A Meadow's Story

A long meadow
stretches to the far mountains
that act as a rim to the Chama Valley,
eons ago an inland sea.
Dinosaurs called the place home.

Today, we tremble at the thought
of our own extinction,
caused not by an asteroid
but by ourselves.

The Mountain Speaks

I stood for a long time before the mountain,
hoping it would speak. After a time,
the mountain spoke to me
in a tongue I did not know
I already knew. It spoke of time
and transience. I asked
the mountain to stay forever.
It replied that it could not,
that even a mountain had to bow
to forces stronger than itself.
The mountain asked me to be content
with the time we had together,
and to let even a mountain
turn to dust.

Time and Stone

Canyons and mesas,
mountains and valleys,
steep cliffs and detritus—
silent rocks tell stories
of hundreds of millions of years,
the secret of time in stone.

Awe brings me here
year after year,
to stir my imagination,
to uncover with reverence
the footprint of time.

"I am part of this," I tell myself,
"and all this is part of me."
I give myself over
to my geology,
and offer thanks to be able
to witness this at all.

Nightfall at Ghost Ranch

Shadows deepen in the mesas' folds,
lengthen east of a row of cottonwood.
The Pedernal and companion mountains
turn ash gray at dusk.
Time for night to settle.
Darkness is not permanent.
The Pedernal will be among the first
to greet the sun.

Urgency

I study the mesa's face—
its blinding brilliance
in afternoon;
its ever-changing,
ever-vanishing colors
in evening;
the lone juniper lodged
in a fortuitous crevice.
My thirsty eyes drink in
a scene that will soon
disappear into memory
and fade into night.

Beneath Old Cottonwoods

Old cottonwood trunks,
deep-furrowed,
ascend toward early spring.
Flawless blue sky descends
almost within grasp.

Ten thousand tiny green fans
flutter to the beat
of a still chilly wind.
I sit motionless
under my cottonwood awning.

In this place,
eternity reaches low.

Mesa

Every mesa has its talus—
rubble at the foot of majesty.

Sandstone cliffs that tell of
time
yield to time.

What would I think of
a mesa without its shards?
Do they not both glow
at sunset?

I scaled the mesa's face
with my eyes –
they told me
Prominence and ruins are one.

The Stream

If a stream winds through all this . . .
it will not
Say where it has been.
— John Ashbery.

Neither particle nor wave,
a stream is pure time,
has no desire but to flow.

It carries dirt;
it cures driftwood;
it cuts through rock.

A stream bows
only to gravity,
taking with it
where it has been
to where it is going,
and picks up more
along the way.

A stream says
where it is going—
it never asks.

Stubborn Old Farmhouse

Beneath the dubious shade
of two scrawny mesquite,
a weathered farmhouse
gathers another splintery coat
of high desert sun.

Old paint peels;
a tin roof tarnishes;
wind scours wood
down to the bone.

Never mind
no one lives here
anymore—
hasn't in decades;
the old stubbornness
is in the wood.

Who tears down
balding memorials
to a folk who scratched
sustenance from so
ungiving a place?
What is our thoroughbred wage
to they who did not
have papers for their breeds?

I petition the mesquite
With a prayer:
Give this dry wood
A little shielding
From the sun.
It doesn't ask for much—
it never did.

Viewpoint

Cerro Pedernal, a mountain
nested in a bed of cottonwood,
a perfect partial frame,
happenstance of perspective
across an alfalfa field.
Stubby, flat-topped volcano,
prized by Georgia O'Keeffe,
once hers, now mine—
she painted, I write,
an inexhaustible mountain,
never twice the same.
I never know when
the Pedernal will surprise me again,
a welcome ambush,
always there to greet me
upon my eager return.

Reckoning Time

Everything
here sprawls—
mesas, buttes, desert valleys,
cottonwood roots, sky;
They tell the same story
of reckoning time:
luminescent canyons
that glow in a low sun;
high desert
that was once a sea.
In this place
intrepid life grows
where it can
and asks for little
in return.
Space is the mask
of sprawling time.

Before Sandia Mountain
for Ed Knop

Mysterious mountain,
sacred to Pueblo tribes,
towers above the desert.
Forested on the east side,
its sheer drop on the west
glows iridescent red
when the sun sinks low.
It draws me near
as I pass it by.
A sublime aura surrounds it—
there is power in this place.
Its power flows
to anyone who will receive it.

Sovereignty in the Mesas

The lord of the mesa reigns
The lord of the mesa remembers
The lord of the mesa reveals

Metaphors of sovereignty
dwell in mesas like spirits,
emanate from mute stone—
tell of sandstone's long dynasty,
dominion's ruddy glow
at sunrise and sunset.
Enthroned in majesty,
mesas crown the long valley
beneath their steep faces—
time's serene nobility
embedded in rock.

Landscape and Dreamscape

High desert, northern New Mexico—where you can touch
metaphors and they return as visible landscape; where massive
sandstone mesas and shining cliffs hint that space manifests
time, and time is medium for space; where over 200 million years
of fossil history chant hymns and tell stories of life long ago;
where aged cottonwood and ponderosa pine dwell happily
among the long-dead but still firmly planted skeletons of
mesquite and juniper; where remnants of an equatorial inland sea
sing graceful *bel canto* to the text of today's scorching summer sun
and bone-dry stream beds.

What sort of landscape is this—where you can touch metaphors
in buttes; where everything firm is allusion; where figures of
speech usher forth from the yellow flowers of the hardy chamisa;
where boundless sky that encloses the badlands opens lungs for
deep breathing and eyes for deep seeing?

Am I seeing? Am I dreaming? Must I choose? If mesas and
pinnacles are vast painted canvases on my soul, are my
words ekphrastic script on a Möbius strip, where high desert and
its indwelling presence undulate seamlessly on a single surface;
where at one moment a deep gorge is geology and geography, in
the next moment pigment and brush, then back again; where
doxology incarnates time as it assumes the form of Bach fugue
and *Magnificat*—*Sicut erat in principio, et nunc, et semper, et in saecula
saeculorum.* Amen.

In these badlands, call and response resonate, amplify each other,
become each other—poem as world, world as poem, at once
impossible and manifest, landscape and dreamscape continuous,
on this Möbius strip of life.

Intimate Immensity

after Gaston Bachelard and Lesley Poling-Kempes

*". . . a sense of shelter and exposure,
enclosure and expansion . . . universal and
personal, dangerous and comforting,
temporal and transcendent."*
—Lesley Poling-Kempes, Ghost Ranch

Inexhaustible space, this sea
of high desert I could melt into.
I take little comfort in the
radiance of the Milky Way
when I no longer know where I am
or the path to where I thought
I was going—
terror so close of kin to awe.
I am lost in this emptiness,
and despair of ever again
being found.
So vast, this wilderness,
Enclosed by tall mesas.
My soul sprawls here,
held in the arms
of these primeval stones.
Beneath a riot of stars,
I take comfort in an expanse
too vast for my imagination
to wrap itself around—
as if being lost is a kind of
being found.

Filling In

In the high New Mexico desert
stand plateaus, buttes, and pinnacles;
between them,
vast canyons and valleys—
all that remain of what were once
thick layers of stone,
and at their summit, an inland sea.
Erosion is time's final judgment
upon the upward thrust
of invisible plates.
Even mountains are mortal.

I view this void from the long valley below;
I can almost feel the slow, indomitable
attrition of stone by ice, snow, rain, and wind.
As if by magic, my eyes fill in what history
    has erased.
If only for a moment, I reverse time.

Dead Cottonwood

On the edge of a stream
stands a cottonwood,
dead for forty years.
Its branches jut into the sky
like a fist. Grass fires
and lightning strikes
have scarcely charred it.
It stands silent watch
Over vast high desert meadows.
New generations are born
and old generations die
in the aging farmhouse nearby.
If the dead cottonwood could laugh,
it would shriek long into the high desert night.
We look upon it and know
that it will outlast us all.

Music of the High Desert

If a mesa's face could sing,
It would sing in *Glorias*;
It would sing a hymn to time,
To the making of the Earth,
To steep cliffs and ancient stone.

The great sandstone face
Would sing of questions
I could not think to ask;
It would sing in choruses
Of the face behind the mask.

Seeking Eternity

I came here to find
the peace of eternity
in mesas' massive cliffs,
in mountains' evening shadows,
in valleys' scruffy fields,
and in a boundless sky.
I found instead
deep canyons carved by water,
stone statues sculpted
by ice's thaw and freeze.
The might of strata formation
played against a counterpoint of erosion.
I came here seeking eternity;
instead I found relentless time.
I found my peace in paradox:
that in the vanishing
lies the exaltation.

Grandeur

High buttes, deep canyons,
endless valleys—
land and sky
more immense than
my delusions of grandeur
could surpass.
Canyons too vast
to fill with my-self.
Awe rescued me;
to feel dwarfed,
a gift of grace.

What this teacher taught me—
that space is a vessel of time,
that solid rock is illusion,
that matter is fluid,
that particle is but
an instant of wave.

Grandeur is the call;
gratitude is the response.

The Same Mesa

I stand in the grassy lowland,
my gaze fixed upon
the face of a vast cliff before me.

Over many days, over many years,
the face of the mesa
displays many moods, many temperaments,
shaped by the angle of the sun,
the clouds that shade it,
rain, snow, wind, and ice,
even the place where I stand,
transfixed.

The mesa now is never
the same mesa next time—
instead, an inexhaustible place,
an inexhaustible face,
that draws me near
to introduce itself.
I return to stand in its mute presence—
ever renewed by this uncanny stone.

The Gift

Surrounded by the bowl
of mesas in the mountain valley
here below,
and the bowl of sun, moon,
planets, stars, and galaxies
far above,
my eyes join
Heaven and Earth
into a single sphere—

a gift that surpasses
anything I could think
to ask for.
Sometimes grace comes in
the most unexpected shapes.

Particle and Wave

In the mesas and mountains,
a complementarity of particle and wave—
each stratum of sedimentary stone,
an age, a noun; the bridge
between ages, sedimentation,
works like a verb—
both, twins of time, inseparable,
yet each in its own way distinct.
At the bottom of each mesa and butte,
a heap of rock crumbs made by
waves of wind and rain and ice—
once dominion of dinosaurs,
now landscape of their graves,
an unending drama
of existence and perishing,
buildup and breakdown,
fateful dance of particle and wave.

Cornflower Blue

Between sunset and dusk,
A badlands autumn sky
settles into a hush
of cornflower blue,
lingers as I walk alone
on an old dirt road,
wraps itself around me
as a faint chill alights
onto the land below.

Vast beyond measure,
this cornflower blue
appears in the sky
one season a year,
is good to look forward to,
is good to remember,
is good to envelop myself in—
this cornflower blue
time of year.

Stillness

A sea of silence—
between the mesas,
down the long valley,
upward to the stars.
Stillness, a Presence
whose Voice I can hear,
gives reassurance
I am not alone.

A Time to Stop, a Christmas Poem

a time to stop—
a time to put
time's relentless arrow
in *pause*—
a time without punctuation

echoes of the *Big Bang*
will still be there
in the farthest galaxy—
the universe will
continue to expand

a time when Alpha and Omega
are invisibly joined
in a Möbius strip
of one continuous plane—
a surface that turns
in on itself and closes
to start anew—
a pause to quiet
the driven heart

a time to stay in one place
long enough to taste eternity—
a Sabbath to the workaday,
time to redeem time—
when even the ordinary
is sacred
and history and fulfillment
are one.

Cottonwoods Before Winter

Before autumn descends into winter,
the cottonwoods in the high desert streambed
shine golden, as if they glowed from within.
Winter will arrive soon enough,
and the branches will be barren for months.
I linger as I pass the cottonwoods,
as if I could store this sight for winter
the way farmers bale hay in summer
for their cattle in the coming snow.
Memory consoles with a warmth of its own.
It is not only hope for spring
that will get me through the cold.
I will remember the gold of endings,
the gentle rain of cottonwood leaves.
I will be ready to let winter in.

Among My Scrub Oak

leathery leaves
contorted branches

not much for majesty
not much for lumber

long roots for drought
long waits for rain

high desert scrub oak
keep their secret
in carefully guarded rings

tell a story
of craggy defiance—
when most everything
around them dries up,
scrub oak still thrive

Bristlecone Pine,
Great Basin

Silent triumph,
sustained by harshness,
attuned to desolation,
perfect fit
of gnarled arms,
shallow roots,
high desert's killing sun,
deep winter,
and precious little rain.
Despite its trials,
the bristlecone pine
refuses to die.

Tarry, Autumn
Driving to Ghost Ranch

Hold, autumn, hold—
your descent into winter
will be swift enough.
Today's brief burst of color
promises the permanence
only of desire.
Branches spare with
withered leaves
will soon give way to
branches heavy with early snow.
I pause in my lazy gait,
first to behold, then to remember.
Yield, autumn, yield—
when there is no more
holding back.

Overnight

Under night's cover,
a cold front swooped in,
turned green, leathery
scrub oak leaves to
bright, brittle yellow and gold.
Next day, I witnessed
newly flayed leaves
float slowly downward
and be hurtled about
by a strong northwest wind.
Trees swayed widely
as future winter
forced its way in.
Backlit translucent leaves
glowed in afternoon sun.
I could hear Beethoven's
Pastorale symphony
as I watched this change of scene.
I felt privileged to sit
in the audience of this drama
of peril and delight.

Storm Among the Mesas

If a sky could be angry, this one would—
bands of gray and black clouds
pass swiftly in front of each other;
in their midst hang
bizarre misty nebulas,
while full udders of moisture
reach toward the ground.

In a sudden conjunction
of light and prism,
sun and rain align themselves
to produce a rainbow
that arcs high into clouds,
then descends and hovers
over the face of the mesa.

Busy indoors at a meeting,
upon sighting this display of refraction
outside our window,
we push aside our computers
and pads of paper, rush outside
to witness this welcome interruption,
grateful that in the midst of a mountain storm,
so genial a stranger should
show up at our doorstep,
move us to pause our work
and let the stranger in.

Long Valley

Consider the compass of this high desert valley—
breadth, beyond the span of peripheral vision;
length, mountains too far for eyes to focus on.

Here, where I stand among the mesas,
scent of rain, increasing darkness,
long, black fingers stretch toward earth;

far ahead into the valley,
broad beams of sunlight
gleam on stately white cliffs;

deeper still,
mountains vanish into sky.

A single instant, many moods;
my eyes strain to hold all this
in a single trope.

Cottonwood Ode

For Ed Knop

Along a streambed,
cottonwood roots claw deep
in search of water
for when the stream cracks dry.
Their trunks' tough bark,
a mail of armor, fends off
wind and rain, snow and ice,
and unforgiving summer sun.

Leaves shimmer brilliant yellow
against the autumn sky.
Majestic cottonwood—
a silent tale in wood and leaf,
of survival and of victory,
in a land that makes no promises.

Void

A deep, wide canyon stretches
between tall mesas and mountains;

in its space, sky begins;
sometimes, it bestows comforting stillness;
other times, fierce storms
assault the valley without warning.

Imagination fills in
what erosion took away.
Sandstone buttes and spires
preserve geology's memory.

This place is not forsaken—
in its basin, time dwells
and never leaves.

Night Music Among the Mesas

In the valley of the mesas,
night draws its ruddy curtain
upon the grassland stage
as the black sky-drape opens
to a pleroma of singing stars
in a double chorus
four-part fugue
Bach wrote in Leipzig—
passion of earth-sky,
in no hurry
for morning and the sun.
Night's parted veil stays open
as long as it can,
until the turning earth
compels a change of scene.
The curtain closes at dawn,
and the celestial choir
retires until night again returns.

Desolation

Where badlands stretch
To the vanishing point,
Immensity is not desolation,
The wrong metaphor
For the story this place tells.
Space is an eyeblink of time—
The sculptor who carved this place.

Here vastness is not barren;
Its gorges are thick with history—
Hundreds of millions of years
Designed this space, once
A tropical inland sea teeming
With dinosaurs and ferns.

Imagination sees
What eyes cannot.
Close our eyes;
Our vision will improve.
Inner space fills the reach
Of the valley between mesas.
What is absent from sight,
Memory can restore
To the Piedra Lumbre basin
In the dwelling places among
Mesas and buttes and spires.

View From a Spire

Tall spires preside over
a high desert valley—
witness fierce storms
rage their way through canyons,
stand watch over windless winter nights
in the glow of the Milky Way.
They observe seasons take their turn
as Earth encircles the sun,
and embed millions of years
in their sandstone strata.
Topped by basalt capstone,
chiseled by erosion,
these spires will one day tell stories
of our time in their midst.
They will capture our tracks
in their solidified mud.
Spires may be made of rock,
but they are not mute.

Furrows

Ruddy furrows,
Sometimes mud, sometimes stone,
In parallel rows
On mountain foothills,
Beneath tall buttes—
These sandstone gullies
Carry time as well as water
In rivulets
Carved by each new rain.
Rain shapes the furrow,
And the furrow directs the rain.
Do they, then, sculpt each other?
Each cause an effect;
Each effect a cause?
Transient trenches
Give away the fate
Of more noble buttes
That rest upon them
Like a crown.
All kingdoms
Eventually fall,
Just as all bleeding
Eventually stops.

Illusions

In the high desert valley
between mesas,
expanse is fulfillment;
wasteland is illusion.
Space incarnates time,
which is here in abundance.

These badlands teem with life,
if you know how to look.
Just because you cannot see
does not mean it is not there—
it is a matter of attending
to what is already Present.

Liquid

High desert valley
surrounded by rock—
siltstone, sandstone,
mudstone, limestone,
making mountains, mesas,
buttes, spires, canyons
that all look permanent—
are they not exactly
as I saw them last year
and ten years before?

These citadels of stone
are tricksters to the eye;
to geologic time's
deposits and erosions,
all rock is flow.
Solid is illusion;
these rocks are liquid—
as is time.

Aeons

I come here every time
to imagine the unimaginable—
steep mesas and deep canyons,
a history book in rock
two hundred million years old—
and I dare to stand unafraid
on sacred ground.
Wonder teaches me
I belong in this place—
I do not disappear into insignificance,
but bear witness to
a scale where
unimaginable becomes possibility,
and I can hold aeons
in the embrace of mere mind.

Mesas and Meadows

Two hundred million years
pass in a fleeting second.
One moment, dinosaurs roam
equatorial marshlands;
in the next, high desert meadows
carpet the valley
with grasses, hay fields, cattle,
and tall stalks of yellow chamisa.
What is this mind
that can travel faster
than the speed of light,
and discern time
in a glance at tall strata
of ancient mesas?
I do not know which
is the greater marvel:
the rapid change of hues
in the setting sun
or the ability to notice it at all.

Story of Time

Ancient buttes and mesas
tell the story of time,
of long crescendo buildups
and staccato breakdowns,
ages that measure our lives
by the history of the Earth—
enigmatic time,
exalted time,
time beyond time
in a story told by stone.

Let Go the Day

Nightfall—
sunset, twilight, dusk.
Cliff faces fade,
vanish from view.
There is always tomorrow
to finish today, to complete
the thought begun yesterday.
Or maybe completions and
new beginnings are only
chimeras of desire and dread.
Maybe for now it simply is time
to let go of the day
and let night fall—
to trust day will come again,
not as return but as possibility.
Maybe it is time to extinguish
the light, and to let in the night.

In Preparation

I am in preparation,
but I know not what for,
or what readiness will look like
once I have arrived.

I dream in metaphor;
what can I know but
familiar metamorphosis
to fill the gulf
between preparation
and destination?

"Larva, pupa, butterfly,"
I utter in magical incantation;
I seek some formula
for this tribulation
of an old body withering
on a vine I do not own.

I turn to thoughts
of preparation:
to bearing witness,
or to being consumed
by what I see.

Writing the Same Poem

It is the same poem,
the same sentiment,
written with different lines,
a yearning that could
fill an ocean and still
spill over onto land.
Dante's Beatrice,
and Faust's Margarete,
where do I find you
or even begin to search?
Compelling as breathing,
you draw me toward you
in the no-place of time
and timelessness.

I am Georgia O'Keeffe
painting her beloved Pedernal,
with the prayer that if
she painted it enough,
God would grant it to her.
What Pedernal do I seek
in poem after poem?
Would I even recognize her
if I were to find her,
and what would
the Recognition Scene be like?

What may I rightfully hope
atop this quicksand of despair?

Cerro Pedernal

A mountain
nested in a bed of cottonwoods,
a perfect partial frame,
happenstance of perspective
across an alfalfa field.
Stubby, flat-topped volcano,
prized by Georgia O'Keeffe,
once hers, now mine—
she painted, I write.
This, an inexhaustible mountain,
never twice the same.
I never know when
the Pedernal will surprise me again,
a welcome ambush,
always there to greet me
upon my eager return.

Not Enough

No poem is ever enough
To exhaust this
Inexhaustible place—
There is always the next poem,
And the next,
For every mood of the mesa,
Every angle of the sun,
Every shadow distinct
From all others.
These cliffs and canyons—
Living fonts of poems
Waiting to be received.

Leaving Ghost Ranch

Faces and folds of steep mesas
nourish my hunger for perspective.
I stand in awe of you,
spirit in stone.
I cannot stay forever
and sate my soul's craving.
I leave you for another year,
perhaps forever.
Driving out the exit
that was only recently entrance,
I look back one last time,
then hope for the solace
of remembering,
this emptiness a kind
of fulfillment.

Immediacy and Memory

Juniper and mesquite,
Deep canyons and sandstone cliffs,
The Chama River and Piedra Lumbre Valley,
Embraced by a forever sky—
My companions and kin,
As close to me as I am to myself,
Until I must leave for
Ordinary place, ordinary time,
Vowing to return,
But uncertain I can keep
My promise.

How to transform
Presence into memory,
Knowing I must leave the badlands behind?
Remembering takes over for immediacy,
And will have to suffice,
Though it never can
Soothe the sting of your absence.
I had never thought to grieve.
Old rock and dead tree
And hardscrabble land—
They would grant me new life,
If only I could return.

Sources

"A Time to Stop, A Christmas Poem," *Dove Tales: An International Journal of the Arts,* "Nature," 2015: p. 92.

"Aeons," *Friday's Poems/Ascent Aspirations Magazine.* http://www.davidpfraser.ca/fridays-poems.html January 26, 2018. Accessed 25 January 2018.

"Among My Scrub Oak," *Songs of Eretz Poetry Review.* 31 January 2018, Accessed 31 January 2018. http://www.songsoferetz.com/

"Beneath Old Cottonwood." Unpublished.

"Bristlecone Pine, Great Basin," *Friday's Poems/Ascent Aspirations Magazine.* 16 December 2016. http://www.davidpfraser.ca/fridays-poems.html Accessed 16 December 2016.

"Bristlecone Pine, Great Basin," website, High Plains Society for Applied Anthropology. http://hpsfaa.org/resources/Pictures/2016-07-25_0917.png Accessed 25 July 2016.

"Cottonwood Leaves in Autumn," *Songs of Eretz Poetry Review.* November 17, 2019. http://www.songsoferetz.com/ Accessed

"Cottonwood Ode." *Anthropology Now.* 7(1) April 2015S: p. 15.

"Dead Cottonwood," *Harp-Strings Poetry Journal* 18(1) Summer 2006: 19.

"Desolation," Unpublished.

"Filling In," *Friday's Poems/Ascent Aspirations Magazine.* February 24, 2017. http://www.davidpfraser.ca/fridays-poems.html Accessed 24 February 2017.

"Geology Lesson," *miller's pond poetry magazine* 19(1) Winter 2016. http://www.millerspondpoetry.com/indexphp/issues/indexphp?page=vol19web1 Howard F. Stein Accessed 6 January 2016.

"Getting My Bearings." Unpublished.

"Gift of Stillness." Unpublished.

"Grandeur," *Friday's Poems/Ascent Aspirations Magazine.* 24 November 2017. Accessed 24 November 2017. http://www.davidpfraser.ca/fridays-poems.html

"Illusions," *Friday's Poems/Ascent Aspirations Magazine.* 13 July 2018. Accessed 13 July 2018. http://www.davidpfraser.ca/fridays-poems.html

"Immediacy and Memory," *Friday's Poems/Ascent Aspirations Magazine.* 27 July 2018, Accessed 27 July 2018. http://www.davidpfraser.ca/fridays-poems.html

"In Preparation." Unpublished.

"Inanimate but Not Dead." Howard F. Stein. *Centre and Circumference*. New York: MindMend Publishing, 2018. P. 55.

"Intimate Immensity." *Friday's Poems/Ascent Aspirations Magazine*. February 9, 2018. http://www.davidpfraser.ca/fridays-poems.html Accessed 9 February 2018.

"Landscape and Dreamscape," *Songs of Eretz Poetry Review*. Monday, September 2, 2019. http://www.songsoferetz.com/ September 2019, "Prose Poem" Issue. 2 September 2019. Accessed 2 September 2019

"Leaving Ghost Ranch," *vox poetica*. 26 March 2017. http://voxpoetica.com/leaving-ghost-ranch-nm/ Accessed 26 March 2017.

"Let Go the Day." Unpublished.

"Liquid," *Friday's Poems/Ascent Aspirations Magazine*. 2 February 2018. Accessed 2 February 2018. http://www.davidpfraser.ca/fridays-poems.html

"Long Valley," *miller's pond poetry magazine*. Volume 21, Web 2. Spring 2018. http://www.millerspondpoetry.com/index.php/issues/index.php?page=vol21web2# Howard F. Stein Accessed 30 April 2018.

"Measure," "Skyward," *Songs of Eretz Poetry Review*. 29 January 2018, Accessed 26 July 2018. http://www.songsoferetz.com/2018/01/special-double-feature-measure-ghost.html

"Mesas and Meadows," *vox poetica*. 12 January 2017 http://voxpoetica.com/mesas-meadows/ Accessed 12 January 2017.

"Mesas and Mountains," *Friday's Poems/Ascent Aspirations Magazine*. 7 July 2017. http://www.davidpfraser.ca/fridays-poems.html Accessed 8 July 2017.

"Music of the High Desert," *miller's pond poetry magazine*. Winter 2019. Volume 22, Web 1. http://www.millerspondpoetry.com/index.php/issues/index.php?page=vol22web1# Howard%20F.%20Stein Published 6 January 2019. Accessed 6 January 2019.

"Nightfall at Ghost Ranch," *miller's pond poetry magazine*. Vol 20, web 1. Winter 2017. http://www.millerspondpoetry.com/index.php/issues/index.php?page=vol20web1# Howard F. Stein Accessed 12 January 2017 (original publication).

"Nightfall at Ghost Ranch." *Friday's Poems/Ascent Aspirations Magazine*. February 10, 2017. http://www.davidpfraser.ca/fridays-poems.html Accessed 11 February 2017.

"Particle and Wave," *AIDPC Connections*. (American Indian Diabetes Prevention Center, Oklahoma City, OK) 4(8)August 2016: p. 2.

"Reckoning Time," *Friday's Poems/Ascent Aspirations Magazine*. 25 August 2017, Accessed 25 August 2017. http://www.davidpfraser.ca/fridays-poems.html (original publication)

"Reckoning Time." *miller's pond poetry magazine*. Volume 20, Web 3, Fall 2017. (Republication with permission of *Friday's Poems*) http://www.millerspondpoetry.com/index.php/issues/index.php?page=vol20web3#HowardF.Stein Accessed 2 September 2017.

"Seeking Eternity," *Friday's Poems/Ascent Aspirations Magazine*. 23 March 2018. Accessed 23 March 2018. http://www.davidpfraser.ca/fridays-poems.html

"Seven Poems From Ghost Ranch," and introductory essay about the personal significance of Ghost Ranch. *vox poetica*. *"the deep dive"* (feature).

http://voxpoetica.com/deep-dive/ 6 May 2019. Accessed 6 May 2019. Poems: "Fugitive Hues," "A Mesa and Its Moon," "Night Music Among the Mesas," "Furrows," "Immediacy and Memory," "Overnight," "Not Enough,"

"Sovereignty in the Mesas," *Friday's Poems/Ascent Aspirations Magazine* http://www.davidpfraser.ca/fridays-poems.html 29 September 2017, Accessed 29 September 2017.

"Stillness," *Friday's Poems/Ascent Aspirations Magazine.* 17 November 2017, Accessed 18 November 2017. http://www.davidpfraser.ca/fridays-poems.html

"Storm Among the Mesas," *Floyd County Moonshine.* 10(1–2) Fall 2018: p. 62.

"Story of Time," *vox poetica.* 26 December 2017, Accessed 26 December 2017. http://voxpoetica.com/story-time/

"Three Layers of Night," *Friday's Poems/Ascent Aspirations Magazine.* 19 January 2018, Accessed 20 January 2018. http://www.davidpfraser.ca/fridays-poems.html

"Time and Stone," *Harp-Strings Poetry Journal* 25(4) Spring 2014: p. 16.

"Urgency," "Cerro Pedernal," and "Cornflower Blue." *Light and Shadow.* 2nd edition. Yukon, OK: Doodle and Peck Publishing, 2018. (Orig. 2016).

"View From a Spire," "The Gift," *miller's pond poetry magazine.* Winter 2018. vol21web1. accessed 5 January 2018. http://www.millerspondpoetry.com/index.php/issues/index.php?page=vol21web1#Howard F. Stein

"Viewpoint." Unpublished.

"Void." *Friday's Poems/Ascent Aspirations Magazine.* 15 September 2017. Accessed 16 September 2017. http://www.davidpfraser.ca/fridays-poems.html 16 November 2019.

Permissions

Friday's Poems/Ascent Aspirations Magazine. Ascent Aspirations Publishing. (permission granted by editor, David Fraser)

"Aeons," *Friday's Poems/Ascent Aspirations Magazine. http://www.davidpfraser.ca/fridays-poems.html* January 26, 2018. Accessed 25 January 2018.

"Bristlecone Pine, Great Basin," *Friday's Poems/Ascent Aspirations* Magazine. 16 December 2016. http://www.davidpfraser.ca/fridays-poems.html Accessed 16 December 2016.

"Filling In," *Friday's Poems/Ascent Aspirations Magazine.* February 24, 2017. http://www.davidpfraser.ca/fridays-poems.html Accessed 24 February 2017.

"Grandeur," *Friday's Poems/Ascent Aspirations Magazine.* 24 November 2017. Accessed 24 November 2017. http://www.davidpfraser.ca/fridays-poems.html

"Illusions," *Friday's Poems/Ascent Aspirations Magazine.* 13 July 2018. Accessed 13 July 2018. http://www.davidpfraser.ca/fridays-poems.html

"Immediacy and Memory," *Ascent Aspirations Magazine. Friday's Poems.* July 27, 2018. www.ascentaspirations.ca http://www.davidpfraser.ca/fridays-poems.html Accessed 27 July 2018.

"Intimate Immensity," *Friday's Poems/Ascent Aspirations Magazine.* 9 February 2018. Accessed 9 February 2018. http://www.davidpfraser.ca/fridays-poems.html

"Liquid," *Friday's Poems/Ascent Aspirations Magazine.* 2 February 2018. Accessed 2 February 2018. http://www.davidpfraser.ca/fridays-poems.html

"Mesas and Mountains," *Friday's Poems/Ascent Aspirations Magazine.* 7 July 2017. http://www.davidpfraser.ca/fridays-poems.html Accessed 8 July 2017.

"Nightfall at Ghost Ranch," *Friday's Poems/Ascent Aspirations Magazine.* February 10, 2017. http://www.davidpfraser.ca/fridays-poems.html Accessed 11 February 2017. First published in miller's pond. Winter 2017.

"Reckoning Time," *Friday's Poems/Ascent Aspirations Magazine.* 25 August 2017, Accessed 25 August 2017. http://www.davidpfraser.ca/fridays-poems.html

"Seeking Eternity," *Friday's Poems/Ascent Aspirations Magazine.* 23 March 2018. Accessed 23 March 2018. http://www.davidpfraser.ca/fridays-poems.html

"Sovereignty in the Mesas," *Friday's Poems/Ascent Aspirations Magazine* http://www.davidpfraser.ca/fridays-poems.html 29 September 2017, Accessed 29 September 2017.

"Stillness," *Friday's Poems/Ascent Aspirations Magazine.* 17 November 2017, Accessed 18 November 2017. http://www.davidpfraser.ca/fridays-poems.html

"Three Layers of Night," *Friday's Poems/Ascent Aspirations Magazine*. 19 January 2018, Accessed 20 January 2018. http://www.davidpfraser.ca/fridays-poems.html

"Void," *Friday's Poems/Ascent Aspirations Magazine*. 15 September 2017. Accessed 16 September 2017. http://www.davidpfraser.ca/fridays-poems.html

miller's pond poetry magazine (permission not necessary)

"Geology Lesson," *miller's pond poetry magazine* 19(1) Winter 2016.
http://www.millerspondpoetry.com/indexphp/issues/indexphp?page=vol19web1
Howard F. Stein Accessed 6 January 2016.

"Long Valley," *miller's pond poetry magazine*. Volume 21, Web 2. Spring 2018.
http://www.millerspondpoetry.com/index.php/issues/index.php?page=vol21web2#
Howard F. Stein, Accessed 30 April 2018.

"Music of the High Desert," *miller's pond poetry magazine*. Winter 2019. Volume 22, Web 1.
http://www.millerspondpoetry.com/index.php/issues/index.php?page=vol22web1#
Howard%20F.%20Stein Published 6 January 2019. Accessed 6 January 2019.

"Nightfall at Ghost Ranch," *miller's pond poetry magazine*. Vol 20, web 1. Winter 2017.
http://www.millerspondpoetry.com/index.php/issues/index.php?page=vol20web1#
Howard F. Stein Accessed 12 January 2017.

"Reckoning Time," *Friday's Poems/Ascent Aspirations Magazine*. 25 August 2017, Accessed 25 August 2017. http://www.davidpfraser.ca/fridays-poems.html

"Reckoning Time," *miller's pond poetry magazine*. Volume 20, Web 3, Fall 2017.
(Republication with permission of *Friday's Poems*) http://www.millerspondpoetry.com/
index.php/issues/index.php?page=vol20web3#HowardF.Stein Accessed 2 September 2017.

"Tarry, Autumn," *Miller's Pond Poetry Magazine* 16(2)Spring 2013:
http://www.millerspondpoetry.com/index.php/issues/index.php?page=vol-16-
web2#HowardStein, accessed 6 April 2013.

"View From a Spire," "The Gift," *miller's pond poetry magazine*. Winter 2018. vol21web1.
accessed 5 January 2018. http://www.millerspondpoetry.com/index.php/issues/index.
php?page=vol21web1#Howard F. Stein

vox poetica (permission not necessary)

"Leaving Ghost Ranch," *vox poetica*. 26 March 2017. http://voxpoetica.com/leaving-
ghost-ranch-nm/ Accessed 26 March 2017.

"Mesas and Meadows," *vox poetica*. 12 January 2017. http://voxpoetica.com/mesas-
meadows/ Accessed 12 January 2017.

Seven Poems From Ghost Ranch. The Deep Dive (feature section of journal). *vox
poetica* http://voxpoetica.com/deep-dive/published/posted 6 May 2019. Accessed
6 May 2019.

"Seven Poems From Ghost Ranch," and introductory essay about the personal
significance of Ghost Ranch. vox poetica. *"the deep dive" (feature)*.
http://voxpoetica.com/deep-dive/ 6 May 2019. Accessed 6 May 2019. Poems:
"Fugitive Hues," "A Mesa and Its Moon," "Night Music Among the Mesas," "Furrows,"
"Immediacy and Memory," "Overnight," "Not Enough,"

"Story of Time," *vox poetica*. 26 December 2017, Accessed 26 December 2017. http://voxpoetica.com/story-time/

Songs of Eretz Poetry Review (permission not necessary)

"Among My Scrub Oak," *Songs of Eretz Poetry Review*. 31 January 2018, Accessed 31 January 2018. http://www.songsoferetz.com/

"Cottonwood Leaves in Autumn," *Songs of Eretz Poetry Review*. November 17, 2019. http://www.songsoferetz.com/ Accessed 16 November 2019.

"Landscapes and Dreamscapes," *Songs of Eretz Poetry Review*. Monday, September 2, 2019.

http://www.songsoferetz.com/ September 2019, "Prose Poem" Issue. 2 September 2019. Accessed 2 September 2019.

"Measure," "Skyward," *Songs of Eretz Poetry Review*. 29 January 2018, Accessed 26 July 2018.

http://www.songsoferetz.com/2018/01/special-double-feature-measure-ghost.html

Anthropology Now

"Cottonwood Ode," *Anthropology Now*. 7(1) April 2015: p. 15. With permission of Taylor and Francis.

"Cottonwood Ode" from Howard F. Stein (2015) Poetry, Anthropology Now, 7:1, 129–130,

DOI: 10.1080/19492901.2015.11728314. https://www.tandfonline.com/

Harp-Strings Poetry Journal (defunct)

"Dead Cottonwood," *Harp-Strings Poetry Journal* 18(1) Summer 2006: 19.

"Time and Stone," *Harp-Strings Poetry Journal* 25(4) Spring 2014: p. 16.

Floyd County Moonshine (permission from editor, Aaron Lee Moore)

"Mesas and Their Valleys," *Floyd County Moonshine* 7(1) Winter 2015: 31.

"Storm Among the Mesas," *Floyd County Moonshine*. 10(1-2) Fall 2018: p. 62.

DoveTales: An International Journal of the Arts
(Permission from the editor-in-chief, Carmel Mawle)

"A Time to Stop, A Christmas Poem," *DoveTales: An International Journal of the Arts*, "Nature," 2015: p. 92.

Doodle and Peck Publishing. Yukon, OK.

Howard F. Stein. *Light and Shadow*. 2nd edition, 2018. (Permission from publisher, Marla Jones)

"Urgency," "Cerro Pedernal," and "Cornflower Blue." *Light and Shadow. 2nd* edition. Yukon, OK: Doodle and Peck Publishing, 2018. (Orig. 2016).

Centre and Circumference. Howard F. Stein New York: MindMend Publishing, 2018. (Permission granted from publisher/editor, Dr. Inna Rozentsvit).

"Inanimate But Not Dead," Howard F. Stein. *Centre and Circumference.* New York: MindMend Publishing, 2018. P. 55.

High Plains Society for Applied Anthropology website.

"Bristlecone Pine, Great Basin," website, High Plains Society for Applied Anthropology. http://hpsfaa.org/resources/Pictures/2016-07-25_0917.png Accessed 25 July 2016.

***AIDPC Connections* (American Indian Diabetes Prevention Center, Oklahoma City, OK).**

"Particle and Wave," *AIDPC Connections.* (American Indian Diabetes Prevention Center, Oklahoma City, OK) 4(8)August 2016: p. 2.

About the Author

HOWARD F. STEIN IS AN APPLIED, PSYCHOANALYTIC, MEDICAL, AND organizational anthropologist, psychohistorian, organizational consultant, and poet.

He is a professor emeritus in the Department of Family and Preventive Medicine at the University of Oklahoma Health Sciences Center, where he taught for nearly thirty-five years. During his time teaching clinical behavioral science in rural family medicine residency programs, he fell in love with the wheat and cattle family farming culture of northwest Oklahoma, and came to specialize in rural medicine.

He also is the author or editor of thirty-two books, including ten books or chapbooks of poetry. His most recent books of poems are Centre and Circumference (MindMend Publishing, New York: 2018) and Light and Shadow (2nd edition. Doodle and Peck Publishing, Yukon, OK. 2018). He is Poet Laureate of the High Plains Society for Applied Anthropology, whose annual retreats have brought him to Ghost Ranch for more than twenty-five years. The spirituality and Sense of Place that pervade Ghost Ranch have inspired more than a hundred poems in which he strives to evoke and bring to life the lived experience of its vastness and intimacy.